Test Your Bible Knowledge

The Book of Revelation

Chapters 1-22

By

Ernest Collins

Print information available on the last page

Rev. date: 01/25/2019

To order additional copies of this book, contact:
Xlibris
1-888-795-4274
www.Xlibris.com
Orders@Xlibris.com

Revelation Chapter 1-22

1. List the seven virtues. (Seven spirits).
    -the spirit of the Lord

    -the spirit of wisdom

    -the spirit of understanding

    -the spirit of counsel

    -the spirit of might

    -the spirit of knowledge

    -the spirit of the fear of the Lord

2. How did Jesus make his message known to John?
    -an angel delivered it to John (1:1)

3. Who will see Jesus when He returns?
    -everyone alive plus the dead who crucified Him (1:7)

4. What did God promise to those who read, hear, and keep the word of God?
    -blessing (1:3)

5. Glory brighter than the noonday sun is called **Shekinah glory**.

6. Seven years of God's wrath is called **Tribulation Period**.

7. Thousand year reign of Christ on earth is called **Millennium**. (20:2)

8. The **Seven Lamp stands** symbolizes the seven churches and the seven church period. (1:13)

9. Who is the Great High Priest of the church?
    -Jesus (1:13)

10. What do the seven stars in His hand represent in verse 11?
    -the angels of the seven churches

11. Which church was commended because of its soundness of faith and its perseverance through persecution?
    -Ephesus (2:2-4)

12. This group was probably a libertine sect who attempted to use Christian liberty as an excuse for self indulgence and immorality.
    -Nicolaitans (2:6,7)

13. List the Heavenly Crowns for overcomers.
    -the incorruptible crown (1 Cor. 9:24-27)

    -the crown of rejoicing (1Thes. 2:19,20)

    -the crown of life (James 1:12, Rev. 2:10)

    -the crown of righteousness (2 Tim. 4:8)

    -the crown of glory (1Peter 5:2-4)

14. The first four church letters were addressed to:
    -Ephesus

    -Smyrna

    -Pergamos

    -Thyatira

15. Who was the false priestess in Thyatira leading people from God?
    -Jezebel (2:20-24)

16. What are the two deaths? How do they differ?
    -First and second deaths

    -First is physical and second is spiritual (20:5, 14, 2:11)

17. What does a compromising church need to know?
    -that Jesus yields a sword called the Word of God (2:12)

18. Who used the women to entice the children of Israel into idolatry and fornication?
    -Balak (2:14, 15)

19. Who is described as having eyes of fire and feet of bronze?
    -Christ (2:18)

20. Who burned the scriptures?

   -Diocletian

21. What are the Bible's three R's?

   -Remember (Rev. 2:5, John 15:20) Repent (Rev. 2:5, Luke 13:3,) Be Righteous (1 Tim. 6:11, 12)

22. What false reputation did the church at Sardis have?

   -They had reputation of being alive but were really dead (3:1)

23. How does one avoid being lukewarm?

   -be earnest, repent, and open the door to your heart (3:19,20)

24. What is the worst state for a Christian to be in?

   -lukewarm, neither on fire for the Lord nor ignorant of Him (3:15,16)

25. What are the last three churches?

   -Sardis, Philadelphia, Laodicea

26. Why was the church at Philadelphia so weak?

   -several of the church members were not true believers (3:9)

27. Which letter probably applies to today's church?

   -Laodicea 3:14)

28. What is called a period of testing, another name for the Tribulation Period?

   -Hour of Trial (3:10)

29. What did Jesus promise those who overcome? (3:12,13)

   -I will make you a pillar in the temple of My God

   -Never again will he leave it

   -I will write on him

30. What door is Jesus talking about in verse 20? Who can open the door?

   -the door of the Church; it is opened by individual believers

31. What are the Four Doors of Revelation?

-the door of opportunity for evangelism and missionary (3:8)

-the door of one's heart for salvation (3:20)

-the door of Heaven for the rapture (4:1)

-the door of Heaven for the second coming (19:11)

32. What theory begins with God creating the heavens and earth in six days and resting on the seventh?

-7,000 year theory

33. Why was John called into heaven?

-to see the things that must be here after (4:1)

34. Who are the twenty four elders? What will they wear in heaven?

-they seem to be angelic beings whose function is to worship and serve God; they will be dressed in white (4:4)

35. What do the four living creatures resemble?

-Lion (king of beasts) - the Gospel of Matthew calls Jesus the king of the Jews

-Ox (beast of burden) - the Gospel of Mark calls Jesus a servant

-Man (human) - the Gospel of Luke calls Jesus the Son of Man

-Eagle (rules the skies) - the Gospel of John calls Jesus, God

36. What do the blazing lamps before the throne represent?

-the seven spirits of God (4:5)

37. What stones describe the appearance of the one on the throne?

-jasper and carnelion (4:3)

38. Who are the angels that guarded the throne of God?

-Seraphim and Cherubim (4:3)

39. What did John use to describe what he saw, since human words could not?

Symbols

40. Give six examples of the Rapture.

    1. Enoch (Gen, 5:24) He went to heaven without first dying.

    2. Elijah (2Kings 2:11) He was walking on earth when he was suddenly taken up into heaven.

    3. Jesus (Acts 1-9) Jesus was taken up into the clouds to heaven.

    4. Philip (Acts 8:39) Philip was taken away, but then reappeared in another location.

    5. Paul (2 Cor. 12:1-4) Paul was caught up into heaven, and then later returned to earth.

    6. Two Witnesses (Rev. 11:3-12) After being killed, they will rise from the dead and ascend into heaven

41. One who shares in the inheritance of others is called

    joint heir

42. Why did John weep? (5:3)

    Because no one was found who was worthy to open the scroll or look inside

43. Why was it necessary for one of the elders to comfort John? (5:3-5)

    Because John had lost sight of the victory of the Lamb and this always results in hopelessness and tears.

44. What is this scroll?

    The scroll contains the record of God's judgments, long since made but now to be enacted (5:1,2)

45. Who told John to stop crying?

    One of the 24 elders (5:3-5)

46. What is the implied significance of the scroll?

    The destiny of all mankind will be affected by the scroll (5:1,2)

47. When heaven is singing to Jesus, what will all creatures on earth and under the sea do?

    Will sing praise to him (5:13)

48. How are the comings of Jesus symbolized in John's vision?(5:12)

    The first time he came as a Sacrificial Lamb

    The second he will come as the Tribe of Judah

49. Why is the Church a royal priesthood?

    Have been a kingdom and priests to serve our God (5:10)

50. Who foretold that he would be as a lamb led to the slaughter?
    Isaiah (Isaiah 53:7)

51. What is the teaching or beliefs about end time called?
    Eschalogy

52. What weapon did the rider on the white horse carry?
    A bow but no arrow (6:2)

53. When does the Tribulation Period begin?
    When Christ open the first of the seven seals (6:1)

54. Seven Years of God's wrath is called
    Tribulation Period (6:1)

55. Thousand year reign of Christ on earth is called
    Millennium

56. What do the seals represent? (6:1)
    Represent the beginning of Christ's judgment of unbelievers on the earth during the Tribulation Period

57. Which seal brings war and a lack of peace?
    2ⁿᵈ seal (6:3,4)

58. Which seal brings death to a fourth or the population of the Earth?
    Fourth seal (6:7, 8)

59. What is the name of the rider on the pale horse and who was following him?
    Death, followed by Hades (6:8)

60. How much will a quart of wheat cost during the Tribulation Period?
    The equivalent of a day's wages (6:6)

61. Who was commanded to hold back their destruction forces until God's servants can be sealed? Why are they doing it?
    The four angels, God is still giving people a chance to repent (7:1,2)

62. Who asked two questions?
   One of the twenty-four elders (7:13)

63. What will the 144,000 preach? Why is their messag so important? (7:10)
   Preach salvation through the blood of the Lamb.
   The Jews will finally accept Jesus as the Messiah.

64. What is the difference between the twenty-four elder and the Tribulation Saints? (7:13,14)
   Twenty-four elders represent Christian of the Church Age.
   The Tribulation Saints are those saved after the Rapture.

65. What is the tribulation that will occur before the Rapture called?
   Post-tribulation

66. The Rapture will occur before the tribulation is called
   Pre-tribulation

67. The Rapture will occur during the tribulation is called
   Mid-tribulation

68. Who were the seven trumpets given to?
   Seven angels (8:2)

69. What signify the righteousness of the believers' conduct?
   Robes (7:9)

70. What signify the victory of the saints over tribulation, which they have under gave for the Lord's sake?
   Palm branches (7:9)

71. What in heaven indicates solemnity?
   Silence (8:`1)

72. What signifies the prayers of the saints, which are brought to God by Christ as another angel?
   The Golden Censer (8:3)

73. What will signal judgment upon the earth?
   The first trumpet (8:7, 8, 9)

74. Which trumpet turn a third of the sea into blood?
  The second trumpet (8:7, 8, 9)

75. Which trumpet makes a third of all fresh water bitter?
  The third trumpet (8:10, 11)

76. Which trumpet takes away a third of the light from the heaven during both day and night?
  The fourth trumpet (8:12)

77. The fragrance of the incense reminds God of what? (8:3)
  The death of His son who died for the sins of the world

78. Why would God call for an earthquake? (8:5)
  To avenge the death of the Tribulation Saints and to symbolize God's wrath

79. What are opened secretly?
  The seven seals (8:2)

80. What are sounded openly?
  The seven trumpets (8:2)

81. When was Satan given the key to the Abyss?
  When the fifth trumpet sounded (9:1, 2)

82. What results in the death of a third of the surviving unbelievers on the earth?
  The sixth trumpet (9:13-15)

83. What is the Abyss?
  A deep pit where demons are kept (9:1)

84. What happen when Satan descend and open the Abyss? (9:2)
  A thick black smoke will rush out, covering the earth in darkness

85. _____ is part animal and part human?
  Locust (9:3)

86. Who asked for the release of the four angels at the river?
  Someone speaking for the martyred saints (9:13)

87. What are some of the Tribulation Period sin? (9:20-21)

  1. Demon worship

  2. Idolatry

  3. Murder

  4. Black magic

  5. Sexual immorality

  6. Theft

88. Who is Abaddon?

  Abaddon means destroyer, destruction. Greek name Apollyon, one of Satan's top henchmen (9:11)

89. What is the belief that trees, stones, and other objects have soul?

  Animism

90. How many mounted troops will kill a third mankind through the three plagues that will come of their horses' mouth?

  200 million (9:16-19)

91. What are the two commissions God gave to all Christian through John? (10:9-11)

  1. To assimilate the Word of God into our lives by doing what the Bible says.

  2. To spread the Word of God to all peoples, nations, languages and kings

92. Who has the voice of seven thunders?

  God (10:3)

93. Who was assigned the task of prophesying about many peoples, nations, languages, and kings by God?

  John (10:11)

94. What happen when John ate the little book?

  It became sweet in his mouth, but bitter in his belly (10:8-10)

95. What is a symbol for the voice of God?

  The Seven Thunders (10:3)

96. What will the glow on the mighty angel's face indicate?

  He has been in the present of the God (10:11)

97. Who will raise his right hand and declare that there will be no more delay for the judgment of the earth?
The angel standing on the sea (10:5,6)

98. Send the nation in to turmoil and confusion is called
Reeling

99. The alter that will be rebuilt was called
The Golden altar

100. What will God do to see how many people on earth truly worshipping Jesus?
God will evaluate (count)

101. What is the large room just inside the door of the temple building called?
Holy place

102. Why will God tell John not to measure the outer court of the temple?
Because it has been given to the Gentiles (11:2)

103. Why will God figuratively refers to Jerusalem as Sodom and Egypt?
Because it will be full of wickedness (11:8)

104. What will cause the world to rejoice during the Tribulation Period?
The death of the two witnesses (11:10)

105. Who will give an adequate testimony for God and against Antichrist?
Two witnesses (11:4-7)

106. Who will make war against the two witnesses and with the saints?
The beast (11:7)

107. What results in the establishment of the millennial kingdom of Christ?
The Seven Trumpet (11:15)

108. What is the last and greatest war before the millennium called?
Battle of Armageddon (Rev. 16:16)

109. What did God empower His two witnesses to do?
Prophesy for 1,260 days (Rev. 11:3)

110. Who represents the Church from Pentecost to the Rapture?
The twenty-four elders (Rev. 11:16-17)

111. Who is clothed with the sun, and the moon underneath her feet, and on her head a crown of twelve stars?
The woman (Rev. 12:11)

112. What are symbols of angels called?
Stars

113. Who or what is the red dragon?
The devil or Satan (Rev. 12:9)

114. When were there wars in heaven?
When Christ overcome Satan through His death, resurrection and ascension (Rev. 12:7)

115. Who is the angel that will cast Satan out of heaven?
Michael (Rev. 12:7)

116. Where will Satan go when he is cast out of heaven? Why will he be so angry?
To the earth, because he has lost his place in heaven (Rev.12:9-10)

117. Who is God's head archangel in battle?
Michael (Rev. 12-7, Jude 9)

118. Who or what is the beast from the sea?
Is an ally or agent of Satan who wars against the saints (Rev.13:1, 2)

119. Who receive what appears to be a fatal wound that will be healed?
The Antichrist (Rev.13:3, 4)

120. Who will give his power and authority to the Antichrist, so the world will be decided and worship the dragon?
The dragon (Rev.13:1-4)

121. How will the False Prophet deceive the unbelievers of the earth?
   By mean of wonders and miracles (Rev.13:13-15)

122. Who will receive the mark of the beast?
   Unbelievers (Rev.13:16-18)

123. Will people be saved during the Tribulation Period?
   Yes (Rev. 13:7)

124. Is the mark your Social Security number, credit card number, or driver's license number?
   No, is the mark, number, or name of the Antichrist (Rev.13:17)

125. What is a symbol of the masses of humanity? What is a symbol of the land of Israel?
   The sea, the earth

126. What is worshiping any gods other than the God of the Bible called?
   Spiritual fornication

127. When will Jesus seal the 144,000 Jewish witnesses?
   Between the opening of the sixth and seventh seal (13:1)

128. What is a symbol of evil spirits or demon possession?
   Maddening wine

129. Who will use his great sickle to gather the wicked nations of the earth?
   The fourth angel (14:17)

130. Who warn the people of the earth to not worship the Antichrist or receive his mark?
   The third angel (14:9-12)

131. Who are ones who kept themselves pure during the Tribulation Period?
   144,000 (14:1-5)

132. List two reasons why many believe the Church will be raptured before the Tribulation Period.
   1. Jesus will rescue us from the coming wrath
   2. God did not appoint us to suffer wrath

133. What is the valley where the Battle of Armageddon will be fought called?
   Valley of Magiddo

134. What began with the seven seals, and will be finished with the seven last plagues?
   The wrath of God (15:1)

135. What will the golden bowls contain?
   The wrath of God (15:1)

136. Why will smoke fill the Temple?
   To keep everyone out (15:18)

137. Who summon the seven angels of God's wrath?
   Four living creatures

138. The gold lid on the Ark of the covenant is called
   Mercy seat (Ex.25:17-22)

139. What produces the destruction of Babylon?
   The seventh vital (16:17-24)

140. Who poured out his bowl on the rivers and springs of water and they became blood?
   The third angel (16:4)

141. Which bowl cause ugly and painful sores?
   The first bowl (`16:2)

142. When will judgments come to an end?
   When the seven bowls of God's wrath are poured out

143. Who tells the angels to pour out the bowls of wrath?
   A voice from the temple (16:1)

144. Who will the blessed be during the Tribulation Period?
   Those who watch for Jesus and keep their garments (16:15)

145. What will the evil spirits do to gather men for the battle of Armageddon?
   Will perform miraculous sign (16:14)

146. Spiritual prostitutes (people) who take up false religion are called
Adulterous

147. Who will commit adultery with the kings of the earth?
The harlot religious system

148. Who is the mother of prostitutes and of the abominations of the earth?
Mystery Babylon the Great (17:5)

149. What is the condition of John when he saw this vision? What does his condition mean? (17:3)
He was in the spirit. He was under the influence of the Holy Spirit

150. Who will cause the beast and the ten horns (kings) to hate and destroy the prostitute?
God (17:17)

151. Who will show John the punishment of the prostitute who sits on the scarlet beast?
An angel (17:1-5)

152. Who will rule with the Antichrist during the Tribulation?
The ten horns (ten kings)

153. What will happen to those in heaven, who suffered at Babylon's hands?
Will rejoice over God's judgment of her (18:20)

154. Why would a heavenly voice call God's people out of Babylon?
So they will not share in her crimes and judgment (18:4-7)

155. What will Babylon use to lead people astray?
Magic(18:23)

156. How many nations have been defiled by Babylon?
All of them (18:3)

157. Who blood will Babylon be responsible for shredding?
The prophets, saints, and all who are killed on earth (18:24)

158. What will be the extent of Babylon's punishment?
She will be paid double from her on cup, given torture and grief to match the glory and luxury she gives herself. She will reap what she sows (18:6,7)

159. What was Babylon's magic spell and does any of it exists today?
Sorcery, astrology, and culture practices. Yes, they exist today (18:3)

160. How long will it take God to destroy Babylon?
One hour (18:17)

161. What comes from a Hebrew word meaning praise the Lord?
Hallelujah (19:1-6)

162. Who fell down and worship God?
The twenty-four elders and four living creatures (19:4)

163. What is the 1000 year reign of Jesus on earth called?
Millennial Kingdom (20:2-7)

164. When will Christ destroy the armies of the earth?
At the battle of Armageddon (16:16)

165. Who will perish at the Battle of Armageddon? (19:21)
All those who take the Mark of the Beast and worship his image

166. Who is the bride of the Lamb?
The Church of Christ (19:7)

167. Who are the armies of heaven? (19:4)
The Church, Angels, Tribulation Saints, and old Testament saints

168. What is the final abode of Satan called?
Lake of fire (20: 10)

169. Who will comprise the fourth army?
The Old Testament Saints

170. Which army will compose of the entire Church from Pentecost to the Rapture?
The first army

171. List the succession of steps narrated to bring to our attention how securely God will imprison Satan for 1000 years.
   1. Laid hold on the dragon
   2. Cast him into bottomless pit
   3. Shut him up
   4. Set a seal upon him (20:3)

172. Which resurrection is called the resurrection of life?
The first resurrection (20:5-6)

173. Which resurrection is called the resurrection of damnation?
The second resurrection (20:14)

174. What are religious people who will hold political positions during the Millennium called?
Political Priesthood

175. What are members of Jesus' family who will work as priests during the Millennium called?
Royal Priesthood

176. Another heaven that will replace the one that now exists is called
New Heaven

177. What is the earth that will replace the one that now exists called?
New Earth

178. Where will Satan repeat what he tried at the Battle of Armageddon?
Battle of Gog and Magog (20:8)

179. Which book is the list of all who were born once (every person who every lived)?
Book of Life (20:12-15)

180. Which book is a list of all who is born twice?
Lamb's Book of Life (20:12-15)

181. Who took John to a high mountain and why?
An angel, so he could see the Jerusalem (21:9)

182. What is meant by universalist?

One who holds to the unbiblical teaching that eventually, all of mankind, including those who have died unrepentant, will be saved

183. What is the New Jerusalem?

It is where God dwells among his people(21:2)

184. What is mainly for the wedding day, while what is for life?

A bride, wife (21:9)

185. List those who will enter the heavenly city (21:8).

1. The cowardly
2. The unbelievers
3. The vile
4. Idolaters
5. The sexually immoral
6. Those who practice magic arts
7. Liars

186. What will be built on twelve foundations and have twelve gates?

New Jerusalem (21:2)

187. What will not have a temple because God and Christ will be the temple?

New Jerusalem (21:2)

188. Why will God create a new heaven and earth?

Because the old ones will pass away (21:1)

189. What happen to those who rejected God during their life time?

Cast into the Lake of Fire (20:15)

190. What is the first layer of the wall's foundation as well as the entire wall of New Jerusalem built with?

Jasper (21:18)

191. What is the first stone in the breastplate of the High Priest?

Jasper (21:18)

192. What will the unrepentant sinner, have their portion in?
In the Lake of Fire (20:10)

193. What will the physical identity of the Holy city include?
River, trees, streets and mansions (22:1,2)

194. What does the water flowing from the throne of God symbolize?
The water refers to the Holy Spirit, it is a symbol of eternal life(22:1)

195. What is the water of life?
Living water, the Holy Spirit (22:1)

196. When John fell down to worship the angel, what did God tell him to do?
John is told to leave his book open(seal not). The Messiah has come His return is imminent and thus the time is at hand (22:8-10)

197. What will believers have on their foreheads in heaven?
The name of God (22:4)

198. What was John's mistake that we read about in chapter 22?
He fell down to worship an angel (22:8)

199. How do we know the words of Revelation are true?
Because John testifies to everything contained in Revelation (22:8)

200. What can a person do to be blessed by God?
He can keep the words of this book by obeying what it says (22:7)

Revelation Chapters 21-22

When God created the present heaven and the earth, He declared that they were very good. Would He say that today? No, He would not say that today, because there is too much pollution of violence hatred devastation, suffering, and pain on earth due to our sin. 2 Peter 3:10, say, "But the day of the Lord will come as unexpectedly as a thief. Then the heavens will pass away with a terrible noise, everything in them will disappear in fire, and the earth and everything on it will be exposed to judgment." God at last brings forth the New World after the thousand years Millennial Age. The chief characteristic of this New Heaven is that it is entirely free from any taint of sin and therefore the resultant effects of sin are absent. He will remove all of their sorrows, and there will be no more death or sorrow or crying or pain. For the old world and its evils are gone forever (Rev. 21:4).

The New Heaven comes into being after the 1000 years, and after the rebellion and the Great White Throne Judgment which follow the 1000 years.

Look at the order of events

1. Rapture: the Church is taken to heaven at Christ return (1 Thessalonians 4:13-18)

2. Tribulation Period: seven years of God's wrath (Rev. 6-19)

3. Battle of Armageddon: the last and greatest war before the Millennium (Rev. 19)

4. Imprisonment of Satan: an angel will seize and bind Satan for a thousand years (Rev.20)

5. Inauguration of the Millennial Kingdom: the 1,000 year reign of Jesus on earth (Matt.25)

6. The Millennial Kingdom (Rev. 20; Isa 11)

7. Satan Is Loosed : the Abyss will be opened one more time, and Satan will be released to resume his old ways (Rev. 20)

8. The Brief Rebellion at the Battle of Gog and Magog Satan will repeat what he tried at the Battle of Armageddon (Rev. 20)

9. Great White Throne Judgment ("Second Death") : God's judgment seat for unbelievers (Rev. 20)

10. New Heaven and New Earth: everything new (Heavenly Realization) Rev. 21-22

11. New Jerusalem (Rev. 21-22)

In the New Jerusalem There Will Be No More:

1. death mourning, crying, or pain (Rev. 21:4)

2. temple (Rev. 21:22)

3. sun or moon (Rev. 21:23)

4. night (Rev. 21:25)

5. impure, shameful, or deceitful thoughts (rev. 21:27)

6. curse (Rev. 22:3)

Printed in the United States
By Bookmasters